# C.F.W. Walther

## Hero of Faith

By Gerald Perschbacher

Illustrated by John Martin

CONCORDIA PUBLISHING HOUSE • SAINT LOUIS

Copyright © 2011 Concordia Publishing House
3558 S. Jefferson Ave., St. Louis, MO 63118-3968
1–800–325–3040 · www.cph.org

Written by Gerald Perschbacher
Illustrated by John Martin
Edited by Rodney L. Rathmann
Editorial assistant: Amanda G. Lansche

Manufactured in Burlington, WI / 034280 / 160010

# Table of Contents

*Young Pastor Ferdinand Walther wonders what life will be like in America.*

# chapter one
# A Young Man Remembers

The sun moved low in the western sky on a cheerless day in winter. A chilly wind whipped against the young man's cheeks as he walked on the creaky deck of the ship called *Johann Georg*. The tall sails of the ship caught the wind, causing the front of the ship to slice through the white-tipped waves of the Atlantic Ocean. The *Johann Georg* gently bounced up and down as it moved forward. With each mile of waves, it found itself closer to America.

This passenger in the long black wool coat, Carl Ferdinand Wilhelm Walther, did not look anything but ordinary as he stood with a plain scarf around his neck and a tall hat pushed firmly on his head. But one day he would become the first president of The Lutheran Church—Missouri Synod! As he stood on the deck, he thought of his home in Germany.

His family and friends had called him Ferdinand when he was young. What trouble he had spelling this long name when he was little! As a boy, he played in the fields near Langenchursdorf—

a town in Saxony, the territory where Martin Luther had also lived. Growing up, Ferdinand had heard many stories about Martin Luther, the great religious reformer.

He heard how Doctor Luther had learned about God's love and forgiveness in the Bible. Ferdinand heard these stories from his father, who was a pastor. His grandfather had been a pastor too. The Walther family knew

*Walther was born in Saxony in what is now known as Germany.*

*As a boy, Walther heard stories about Martin Luther, the hero of the faith who sought to return the Church to the teachings of the apostles.*

Jesus as their Savior; they found joy and purpose in loving and serving God. So Ferdinand grew up learning a good deal about important men in the Christian Church. But Ferdinand did not know he, himself, would become one!

His parents, Gottlob Heinrich and Johanna Wilhelmina Walther, had twelve children. Ferdinand was number 8. He lived with his parents and siblings in a very busy house, with children playing and laughing. Sometimes they cried. Sometimes they studied. They did their chores. Father made sure they read from the Bible and understood each passage. Mother cooked, cleaned, smiled, and sang. Together they gave their children a very good life. Though not wealthy with material things, the family knew the richness of love and faith. They trusted and believed in Christ Jesus.

When little Ferdinand was three years old, he learned a German hymn. In English, it said:

"Jesus, Thy blood and righteousness,
My beauty are, my glorious dress."

*Ferdinand and his brother Otto, both young pastors, plan to come to America.*

Those traveling by ship in
the nineteenth century experienced
close quarters, with little privacy
and few comforts.

The man Ferdinand paused and stood alone on the deck of the *Johann Georg*. He hummed that song while the ship raced to America. Running the song through his mind made him feel close to his beautiful Savior Jesus, who dressed him in forgiveness and grace. Humming the hymn made him feel close to his family. Most of them were staying in Germany. Ferdinand was twenty-seven years old now, and his brother, Otto Hermann Walther, the only other Walther male on the rough voyage, was twenty-nine.

A slight warm breeze touched Ferdinand's face as he looked far off, over the partly cloudy ocean. He thought of other ships that carried his friends who were heading for America. There were 665 people in the entire group. Many came from Saxony. They paid high prices to leave Germany. The wealthy left many possessions behind. The poor had few things to sell to pay for their trip. All wanted to worship God freely in America. Most wanted to own land, start businesses, and have families. They wanted to breathe fresh air. They did not want to worry about Europe's wars and armies. They were pioneers heading to the New World called America, encouraged by exciting thoughts of the adventures that lay ahead. But beneath the excitement, some also worried.

*The birds' behavior signaled to those on the ship that land was near!*

While Ferdinand thought of his days as a boy, he stepped near the edge of the ship and rested his arms on the wooden railing. He saw four white birds flying up high. They dipped down and then zoomed up in the sky. They were riding the wind and looking for food. It was a sign that the ship was coming closer to land! He wondered: Would *his* life zoom high into the sky when he found his future in America?

*Martin Stephan preached boldly against the popular movement within the churches of Germany known as rationalism. Pastors who were caught up in this movement emphasized logical applications at the expense of the real message of God's Word. Such pastors, for example, might review the story of the birth of Jesus during a Christmas sermon but then go on to stress the importance of the proper care and feeding of animals instead of focusing on the significance of the birth of the Son of God and Savior of the world!*

Pastor Martin Stephan, the leader of all the people on the five ships, was far older than the Walther brothers. He preached and taught God's Word clearly and simply, with an emphasis on the Gospel. He had wanted to move to America as early as 1811. Now his dream was coming true. Pastor Stephan made enemies; he also made friends. Those people who traveled with Pastor Stephan trusted him, especially those who came from Dresden, the city in Germany where Pastor Stephan had been a clergyman.

It took five ships to carry all those travelers. They found little privacy crammed below deck on *Copernicus, Republik, Olbers, Amalia,* and, of course, *Johann Georg.* Ferdinand was not lonely; the ships were crowded with many families. In addition to the food they brought with them, families also brought a few less necessary things such as special books, tools, and small items they used in their homes. Some brought tiny but precious heirlooms that had been gifts from their grandparents!

*Some 665 people came to build a new home in America, where they could worship God freely and teach God's Word without interference from rationalist authorities.*

Now and then, Ferdinand went up on the deck of the *Johann Georg* to be by himself. Late in the day, he could be away from the other people who stayed below. He would think. He would pray. His prayers were not only for himself. He prayed for his family, his future, his older brother, Pastor Stephan, and the five ships with all the passengers on them.

*While at sea, Walther and other pastors held classes for young people, teaching them school subjects and the catechism. Throughout his life, Walther remained actively interested in young people. To a group of them he once said: "O my young people, God wants our whole life. He desires . . . the enthusiasm of our youth . . . . He asks us to be His, not when we are bent and broken . . . but already when we are young."*

Ferdinand prayed very often! Maybe that was because he was a young pastor. His father and mother wanted him to be a pastor. This is why they sent him to good schools. At age 10, he had entered the *Gymnasium*, which is the German word for the next level above grade school. Ferdinand had to go thirty miles from home to the town of Schneeberg to continue this education in the Gymnasium, a school somewhat similar to American high schools of today! Long before the days of the automobile, this thirty-mile distance required a day's travel by horse. Fortunately, one of Ferdinand's sisters had married the man who was a leader of the school. These relatives took care of Ferdinand and made sure that he studied his lessons.

When Ferdinand turned 18, he knew it was time for him to choose a university! But, which one? He loved music. Should he become a musician as his life's work?

*Ferdinand studied hard and did well in school. He demonstrated outstanding musical abilities. Once he wrote in his diary, "I feel that I was born for nothing but music."*

Napoleon's army invaded Russia in 1812, shortly after the year Ferdinand was born.

## chapter two
# Ferdinand Finds His Way

The world had changed a good deal since
Ferdinand's birth on October 25, 1811. Emperor
Napoleon of France no longer threatened European
peace. Families in Germany had rebuilt their lives
and their homes. The fear of fighting was fad-
ing. More and more territories in Germany were
making agreements with one another. With more
peaceful time, people began to look forward to
good trading, more money, and better lives!

Though 1829 seemed a good time to go to a
university, the year brought bad things too. Wise
Pastor Ferdinand thought about these as he stood
on that windy deck of the *Johann Georg*. A spray
of saltwater sprinkled his face and made him
blink.

The salt stung his eyes! It reminded him
of unhappiness in Germany. People rebelled.
Students raised serious questions that threatened
their teachers. Leaders feared the consequences
of the new freedoms coming to their people.
Too many freedoms might be dangerous. But
what made Pastor Ferdinand's eyes water even

more was that people were not told the Good News of Jesus Christ, their Savior!

*When does the expression of freedom go too far?*

Ferdinand saw his choice of a university as very important. Since age 8, he had attended schools that did not believe in God as the Bible taught. But he did not lose the strong faith of his father and grandfather. During eight years in the *Gymnasium*, he remained strong in his firm faith in Christ. As Pastor Ferdinand stood on the slippery deck of *Johann Georg*, he recalled something. "I was 19 when I left the *Gymnasium*, and I had never had a Bible or a catechism. All I had to study about God and

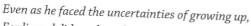

*Even as he faced the uncertainties of growing up,
Ferdinand did not lose the strong faith
in which he had been raised.*

faith was a miserable manual." That manual told about
doing good deeds, not about true forgiveness and faith
in Christ. Instead of teaching from the Bible and the
catechism, Walther's teachers taught from manuals that
emphasized good behavior and responsible citizenship.
Teachers did not present the truth of sin and salvation
in Christ Jesus clearly and boldly, as it appears in the
Bible.

Pastor Ferdinand's thoughts stopped as warmer air lifted off the ocean's surface. The wind pushed him back two steps, and then he regained his balance. He grabbed a wooden railing. His hands now felt damp from the weather and his wool coat warmed him in the mist. The air seemed cheerful and full of promise. Happily, it had lost its "bite."

Cheerful. Happy. It made Pastor Ferdinand think of the past. In 1828, Ferdinand's brother Otto studied theology at the University of Leipzig, making their father happy! Ferdinand wondered, should he also study theology? Then his brother showed him a booklet about a pastor, J. F. Oberlin, written by G. H. Schubert.

*Pastor Oberlin saw people's lives changed by the Gospel.*

Pastor Oberlin changed the lives of people. He did this with the Gospel, the Good News God has for us in Christ Jesus. Pastor Oberlin told people how Jesus Christ suffered and died for them. He told how Christ the Savior was raised from the dead. Christ's life, death, and rising were *for everyone*!

Many people were leaving Europe. Large numbers went to live in America. Not many pastors were going with them. So as people worked to build a new life for themselves in a new land, they found themselves without the comfort of God's Word through preaching and the Sacraments. Pastor Oberlin wanted to preach in America, but the Revolutionary War killed that dream. He never sailed to the New World.

*Pastor Oberlin was kept from coming to America by the Revolutionary War.*

The story of Pastor Oberlin was a turning point in Ferdinand's life. He was not worried about making money. He did not need to be a famous singer or musician. He and his brother would both become pastors!

*Finding it difficult to pastor his congregation according to the teachings of God's Word, Pastor Ferdinand leaves Germany for America together with many congregation members.*

After Ferdinand completed his university schooling, he served as pastor in the small Saxon village of Braeunsdorf. Otto became the assistant pastor to their father in their hometown.

But each wanted more. Several others in the ministry also felt the time had come to leave Germany. Christians in this part of Germany found it difficult to worship God as they chose. America was calling!

The pastor in the long black coat wiped the water from his hands. The chill had lifted. The air smelled fresher. There seemed to be a touch of "green" in it. Ferdinand loosened a few buttons on his coat and reached inside. He pulled out a small notebook, opened it, and read the date: December 31, 1838. New Year's Eve! A day to remember the past. And a day to look forward to the promises of a new year.

*The small island indicated that the ship was on course to New Orleans.*

"Land! Land!" shouted a crewman. He had climbed carefully up one of the masts but had stopped partway in his climb in order to shout the news. The sails seemed to relax. A very small island came into view—no more than a little sand, several large rocks, and bunches of tall grass. But this was what the ship's captain expected to see, providing a sign that the ship was on course. Pastor Ferdinand overheard two crewmen speak. They said it would take five days to reach New Orleans!

*Drawing of the Olbers, one of the five ships carrying the Saxon immigrants to the New World. Travel in the earlier years was dangerous, with many ships and their passengers lost at sea.*

It had been a long, stormy trip across the Atlantic, Pastor Ferdinand recalled. Five ships left Germany to carry people to America in what later became known as the Saxon immigration. *Copernicus* led the way as the first ship to leave among the five. *Johann Georg* was the second ship to set sail just hours later from Bremerhaven, Germany, on November 3, 1838. Now New Orleans soon would be in sight. Later, Pastor Carl Ferdinand Wilhelm Walther would learn that *Copernicus* had arrived five days ahead of *Johann Georg*. *Copernicus* moved faster because of its construction, the crew, winds, and shifts in ocean currents.

*Tragically, the* Amalia *and all the emigrants on board were lost at sea.*

While this man in the damp, dark coat stood facing the wind on that December day, he smiled. He had made the correct choice. The Gospel was his life! America was his future! He was certain that God, his heavenly Father, was happy with that choice.

## Did You Know . . . ?

- The five ships leaving Germany as part of the Saxon immigration include *Copernicus, Johann Georg, Republik, Olbers,* and *Amalia.*

- Very stormy weather struck European waters early in the trip, between November 28 and 30, 1838. Because of this, the *Amalia* sank with a loss of over 55 passengers.

- Pastor C.F.W. Walther was one of approximately 140 passengers aboard *Johann Georg.*

- The immigrants included several other pastors and future pastors, doctors, lawyers, maids, businessmen, craftsmen, and farmers.

- The last of the five ships to land in America was the *Olbers* on January 20, 1839.

Walther celebrated twenty-five
years in the ministry in 1862.
The celebration brought
joy during trying times.
Americans were at war
with other Americans as
the Civil War raged on.

## chapter three

# Overcoming Trials and Struggles
# with the Help of God

Friends of C. F. W. Walther gathered in 1862 for a party! They helped Walther celebrate completing twenty-five years as a pastor! Walther proved to be a very gifted teacher of the Bible, having written hundreds of pages on the subject! He told many thousands of people about the Good News of Christ!

As friends smiled and shook his hand, Pastor Walther recalled key events. He knew how people had helped him in America. He was thankful for people in Germany who also prayed for his work. Walther found America to be a "mission field" for the Gospel of Christ.

At Walther's party people did a lot of talking. They made speeches too. But here and there, as someone spoke, Pastor Walther daydreamed. His mind looked to the past.

He remembered 1839. Pastor Stephan gathered the members of the group of German Lutherans when the four ships finally landed in New Orleans. Pastor Walther was among the leaders. The people took four steamboats up the Mississippi River. The winter weather snipped harder on exposed skin than it had as the people traveled on the ocean. The "deck" passengers were provided with hot water three times a day and were required to prepare their own meals. Large chunks of ice floated down the river, making it dangerous for boats to travel. Ice could poke holes in the ships. They could sink! But God was with them, and they landed safely. The last boat came to St. Louis, Missouri, on February 19.

*The Saxons landing in St. Louis in 1839.*

Why did they go to St. Louis? St. Louis stood as the biggest city on the edge of pioneer territory. Near St. Louis land was available! Hunting was plentiful! The climate was similar to Germany! And here, plenty of fresh drinking water could be found! All these wonderful things were told in a book written by a German named Gottfried Duden. He came to America to be a farmer in 1824. Then he wrote his very popular book and returned to Germany. The book gave hundreds of pages of ideas about the beautiful and bountiful Midwest! He said St. Louis was the city where Germans should go!

*This rendering is based on a painting by G. H. Hilmer.*

The book worked. St. Louis had about 5,000 people in 1830. In 1839, there were 16,500 living there! Many more people came to St. Louis and then moved out West. St. Louis was the gateway to their futures. Pastor Walther remembered the feeling.

Imagine, hundreds of Germans coming to St. Louis all at once! Early in 1833, there had been only eighteen German families living there. By the end of 1834, several hundred Germans lived there. Thousands came later. But this group of Germans arriving in 1839 was different. They had come to America because of their belief in God. They wanted to worship Him in truth and purity.

*St. Louis as it looked in 1840.*

It stabbed Pastor Walther in the heart that not everyone in the city welcomed the Saxon Lutherans, as they soon were called. Store owners and hotel keepers liked the business they brought. But the Germans who had come to town earlier viewed this new group from their homeland with suspicion.

*Not everyone gladly welcomed the immigrants at first.*

Their leaders said mean things about the Saxons and the German newspapers in St. Louis printed these evil words. These things were not true! Some earlier German settlers knew it and quietly helped the Saxons.

Pastor Walther turned his mind back to the party. As it continued, he smiled, talked a little, shook more hands, and then sat in a chair to listen to more speeches. All this made him feel good, but he wanted everyone to give thanks to God for the blessings of twenty-five years as a pastor! Once more, Pastor Walther thought about the past.

About 120 of the Saxon Lutherans stayed in St. Louis in 1839. They formed Trinity Lutheran Church, with Pastor Otto Hermann Walther as its leader. The rest of the Saxons made settlements in Perry County, Missouri, about 100 miles to the south.

*First came sickness and then disillusionment with their leader. Imagine how sad and despondent the colonists must have felt!*

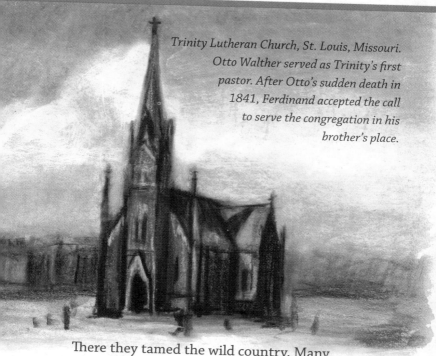

*Trinity Lutheran Church, St. Louis, Missouri. Otto Walther served as Trinity's first pastor. After Otto's sudden death in 1841, Ferdinand accepted the call to serve the congregation in his brother's place.*

There they tamed the wild country. Many became ill, including Pastor Ferdinand Walther. He was so ill that when his brother died suddenly in St. Louis in January of 1841, he could not preach at the funeral! Another German pastor did that. He was Pastor G. W. Wall of an Evangelical Protestant church, which was mainly Lutheran. However, Pastor Ferdinand Walther was not sure what that congregation really believed. During Ferdinand's lengthy illness he studied the Scriptures. God worked through Ferdinand's studies to prepare him for the debate, soon to take place, that would direct the future of the colony.

*In what became known as the Altenburg Debate, Lawyer Marbach and Walther explored two perspectives on the question "Are we still a church?" Walther's argument that God builds the true Church on His Word and the Sacraments carried the day. After the debate, Marbach agreed that Pastor Walther was right and put his agreement in writing.*

There were problems in Perry County. Pastor Stephan did not live as a pastor should! Accused of improper actions, Martin Stephan, leader of the immigrant colony, was removed from his position as leader and then from the colony itself. He was taken across the Mississippi River to Illinois, where he lived the rest of his life.

Some of the Saxon Germans wondered. Was it wrong to come to America? Should they return? Pastor Walther said no! He spoke strongly about staying in America. Yes, these people believed in the true God. They lived by the words of the Bible. Their church was true to God. God did not go away from them. He was with them!

Most of the Saxons said Pastor Walther was correct. They would stay in Perry County. But Pastor Walther would not stay. He was given a divine call to be pastor at Trinity in St. Louis, to take the place of his brother.

*The log cabin college and Concordia Seminary, St. Louis,*
*as it looked in Walther's day. Ferdinand taught at Concordia*
*Seminary, while also serving Trinity Lutheran Church as its pastor.*

## chapter four
# Pastor, Teacher,
## Writer, Husband, and Father

Pastor Walther recalled that time as though it happened yesterday. The Saxons had always valued Christian education. Soon after arriving in Perry County, three pastors built the building out of logs that housed the first school. One of these pastors dug the well that provided the school with water. After Walther came back to St. Louis, the Lutheran school called Concordia was moved from Perry County and found a new home near what is now Holy Cross Evangelical Lutheran Church in south St. Louis. Walther taught the students who assembled there. The school grew. It became Concordia Seminary.

Maybe you know some people who went to that seminary. Pastor Walther knew many of the students in the early years. He loved each one. He helped them to understand the Bible. He asked them to teach others about God. He helped them learn how to preach.

Pastor Walther saw some of those preachers at his party. It made him smile even more! His work was going on in them.

*Family life in the Walther home. Eventually, six children were born into the Walther family.*

Pastor Walther knew that his wife shared in much of his ministry. Before the party, he looked at his wife, Emilie, the sister of J. F. Buenger, who was a student friend of his. She must have noticed he was looking at her. She lifted her head and showed love in her eyes. To her, Pastor Walther was a man of great faith and a kind husband.

C. F. W. Walther married Emilie Buenger on September 21, 1841, in Perry County. Pastor Walther's brother-in-law, Pastor E. G. W. Keyl, conducted the ceremony. In the years that followed, Pastor and Mrs. Walther had six children. Pastor Walther was sad for a moment when he remembered that two of them died when they were young. Then he smiled a tiny smile. He was glad he had told them of their Savior. He was sure they were in the arms of Jesus!

Der Lutheraner *is first published in 1844. Walther's paper helped to unite Lutherans throughout nineteenth-century America.*

## chapter five

# Leader of Lutherans

Walther glanced over the crowd at his party as though he were looking at a picture of his life. People can do that. Just by being there, they reminded him of many successes and some struggles.

He thought about *Der Lutheraner*, a German newspaper he started in 1844 with the help of Trinity Lutheran Church. The paper clearly told messages from the Bible. In its pages, Pastor Walther wanted to emphasize the following truth:

"God's Word and Luther's doctrine pure
Shall now and evermore endure."

This publication became very popular! It opened doors for others who came to America on their own or with immigrant groups other than the Saxons. Dr. Wilhelm Sihler, a pastor in Pomeroy, Ohio, especially appreciated *Der Lutheraner*. He found it encouraging to know that there were others in America who believed in the same things as the Saxons. Pastor Friedrich Wyneken of Fort Wayne, Indiana, also read the paper.

People in Michigan also expressed interest, including Pastor F. A. Craemer of Frankenmuth. These and others wanted to learn more about Pastor Walther and his church group.

Pastor Walther looked very pleased as he sat at his party. He recalled how God had worked through this paper to bring people together. Meetings were held in 1845 and 1846. Pastors talked about forming a large church! In April 1847, at a special meeting held at St. Paul Evangelical Lutheran Church in Chicago, there began what is known today as The Lutheran Church—Missouri Synod.

Who did those at the meeting select as their first president? Pastor C. F. W. Walther!

*At its founding, the new Lutheran church body named C. F. W. Walther its first president.*

Not everyone had the same ideas in the new church body. Pastor Walther wrestled with the problems. So did others. Emilie Walther joined her husband in prayer asking God to bless the new Lutheran church body. As time went on, God's blessing fell upon this group of believers. They came to realize that they wanted to walk in the same way—the way of the Cross, the way of God, the way of the Savior.

Pastor Walther's thoughts returned to the party as he walked from his chair. He had to speak in a moment. But first, came a long introduction by a friend! He would have enjoyed a pat on his hand from his wife, but Emilie was not near him right now. Still, he knew she was proud of him. Her gentle ways meant very much to him.

As the party continued, Walther thought about conditions in the world at that time. The calendar identified the year as 1862, and Americans found themselves fighting each other in a civil war. Just a year before, Pastor Walther had sent his wife and children to live in Jefferson County, Missouri. He sent his family to the safety of the country because more battles and shootings occurred in Missouri during the opening months of war than in any other state.

Pastor Walther knew of the details. He also knew of President Lincoln, who had spoken to many Germans now in America. Mr. Lincoln debated Stephen Douglas in 1858 in Alton, Illinois, a short distance from St. Louis. Mr. Lincoln said that America should offer freedom for "people everywhere, the world over—in which Hans, and Baptiste, and Patrick, and all other men from all the world, may find new homes and better their conditions in life."

Pastor Walther was certain that one day, war will end. A better life will come. However, the war with the devil, the world, and our flesh will continue here on earth. That's why the Church remains so necessary!

With these thoughts, it was timely for Pastor Walther to step forward to the sound of applause and to address the friends at his party.

hero of
faith

# Did You Know . . . ?

- Pastor Wyneken in Indiana came to America six months before the Saxons, but he did not know about them until he read *Der Lutheraner*.

- Pastor Wilhelm Loehe figured prominently in the history of Lutheranism in America, yet he remained in Germany. Pastor C. F. W. Walther traveled back to Germany in 1860 to strengthen his health, to visit with Pastor Loehe, and to ask for more funds to support Lutherans in America.

- Pastor Walther's children were named Christine Magdalene, Hermann Christoph, Konstantin and Ferdinand Gerhard (who were twins), Emma Julie, and Christian Friedrich. Hermann and Christian died as little children. Many young children died in the 1800s!

- While Pastor Walther was president of the seminary and of the Synod, he was also pastor for four church districts in St. Louis. Each considered him to be their founding pastor.

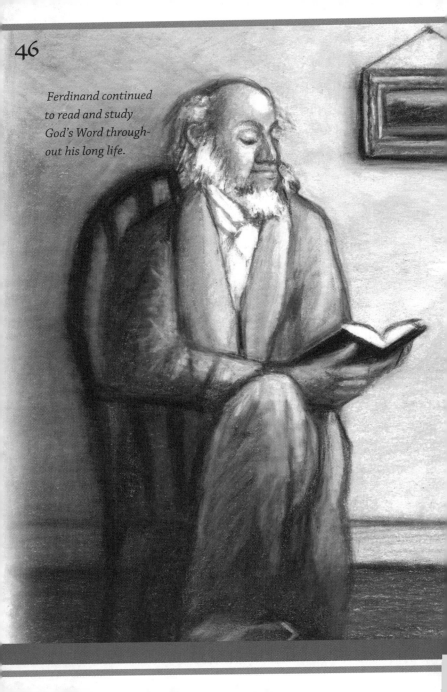

Ferdinand continued to read and study God's Word throughout his long life.

◆ ◆ ◆
## chapter six
# On to Glory

"A person cannot contribute to his becoming alive spiritually. A person cannot convert himself or contribute to it in the least. He is awakened alone by God's power and grace," wrote Walther.

He firmly believed in God as the provider and doer of salvation. He firmly believed in God the Father and Jesus Christ as Savior. He firmly believed in the Holy Spirit. Now, on May 6, 1887, he was preparing to reach the gates of heaven. He still confessed the same belief.

In the years since his twenty-fifth anniversary as a pastor, he had been given an honorary doctorate. He did not want to take it, but it was hard to say no. He smiled as he received it. Then he thanked everyone. He especially thanked God.

Walther still lived in St. Louis. His days as an old man had been spent in studying the Bible. He preached. He taught now and then. He enjoyed students. He had days when he felt good and strong and days when he felt weak and ill. He had been ill many times in his life, but lately it was different.

*Emilie Walther in
her later years.*

His beloved wife Emilie had died two years earlier. His time with her had been too short! How faithful and devoted she had been. How wisely she had managed their household. When she died, his life dimmed. She had no enemies, he said. "My tears flowed plentifully; for what I have lost in this faithful helpmeet cannot be put into words . . . . She, next to God, lived and worked day and night only for me!" He added: "Her memory will be blessed as long as there will be people who knew her."

Dr. Walther visited his adult children in New York and Cleveland, Ohio. He had come for a final visit with them. He felt weak and old. He visited a church conference in Detroit, but became ill. The conference put too much strain on him! In October 1886, he spoke at a convention in St. Louis. Those who heard him were sad. The mighty man of God was nearing his last day!

As Dr. Walther finished his speech, he sobbed. "To God alone be the glory!" he said in Latin. "This must be our life's motto!"

Though difficult, Dr. Walther kept teaching at the seminary. He gave ideas to young people and gave advice to church leaders. Everyone listened!

In October 1886, C. F. W. reached age 75. January 17, 1887, marked his fiftieth anniversary in the Holy Ministry. While his beloved Church was holding a convention in Fort Wayne, Indiana, he lay on his deathbed. By his side was his close friend Professor G. Stoeckhardt, whom he had brought from Germany to follow him as a seminary teacher. The professor asked Dr. Walther if he still believed what he had taught. "Yes," Walther answered!

In those final hours, his life jumped from scene to scene. His memory played pictures as though they were movies. He did not grow weak in his faith!

On Saturday, May 7, 1887, at 5:30 p.m., he entered the realm of heavenly grace and stood before the Savior in glory.

Ferdinand Walther, that young boy who grew up in Germany, had a mission. God filled him with love and energy. He grew to be a young man, ready to share the Word of God in all truth, as Christ proved it. Dr. Walther had many special events in his life. He always gave God the glory, even until his last day on earth.

hero of faith

# Timeline of Events
## during C. F. W. Walther's Life

**1811**   C. F. W. Walther born in Saxony

**1812**   U.S. declares war on Great Britain; Napoleon's army invades Russia

**1819**   Spain cedes Florida to the United States

**1821**   Walther leaves home to attend the Gymnasium

**1825**   Erie Canal opens

**1826**   Pastor Frederic Oberlin dies

**1829**   Walther enrolls in the University of Leipzig to study theology

**1837**   Walther is ordained as a Lutheran pastor; Victoria becomes queen of England

**1838**   Walther leaves as an emigrant for America aboard the *Johann Georg*

**1839**   Log cabin college dedicated in Perry County, MO

**1841** Walther debates lawyer Marbach in Altenburg, MO

**1841** Walther replaces his brother as pastor of Trinity Lutheran Church in St. Louis, MO

**1841** Walther marries Emilie Buenger

**1844** Walther publishes the first issue of *Der Lutheraner* (*The Lutheran*); Samuel F. B. Morse dispatches the first telegraph message from Washington DC to Baltimore

**1846** Neptune discovered

**1847** The Lutheran Church—Missouri Synod begins with Walther as its first president

**1857** Dred Scott decision in U.S. Supreme Court

**1860** Lincoln elected President of the United States

**1868** Cincinnati Reds established (first major league baseball team)

**1876** Alexander Graham Bell invents the telephone

**1887** Walther dies